Dachshund

The Hot Dogger

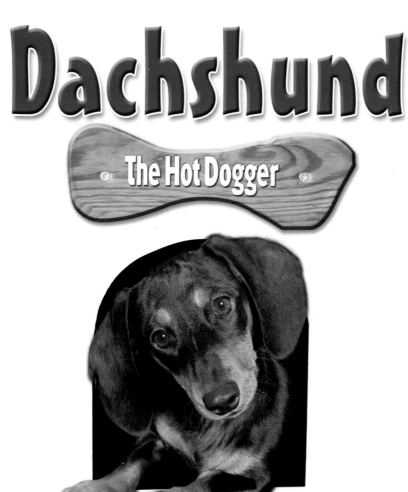

by Natalie Lunis

Consultant: Frances H. (Marci) Forrester
American Kennel Club Judge approved since 1986
and Board Member of the Dachshund Club
of America Board of Directors

BEARPORT
PUBLISHING

New York, New York

Credits

Cover and Title Page, © Cathy Keifer; TOC, © Utekhina Anna/Shutterstock; 4, Courtesy of Los Alamitos Race Track; 5, Courtesy of Los Alamitos Race Track; 6, © Stephen Morton/Getty Images; 7, Courtesy of Los Alamitos Race Track; 8, © Colin Seddon/npl/Minden Pictures; 9, © Andy Rouse/NHPA/Photoshot; 10, © Christie's Images/Corbis; 11T, © Reuters; 11B, © tbkmedia.de/Alamy; 12, © Reuters/Claro Cortes; 13, © Maryann Nash/momsdachshunds.com; 14T, © Henry Ausloos/Animals Animals Enterprises; 14C, © BIOS/Peter Arnold Inc.; 14B, © D.Harms/WILDLIFE/Peter Arnold Inc.; 15, © Ulrike Schanz/Animals Animals Enterprises; 16, © Adoc-photos/Art Resource, NY; 17L, © 2008 Her Majesty Queen Elizabeth II; 17R, Courtesy Liz Kearley; 18, © DAJ/Getty Images; 19, © 2008 PunchStock/IZA Stock; 20, © Astrid Stawiarz/Getty Images; 21, Courtesy of PetEdge; 22, © Per Klaesson/Photolibrary; 23, © Courtesy Liz Kearly; 24T, © Buena Vista Pictures/courtesy Everett Collection; 24B, © James O'Connor; 25, © MGM/Courtesy Everett Collection; 26L, © Roberto Della Vite/agefotostock; 26R, Courtesy Leslie Grimmell/www.eddieswheels.com; 27L, © Lake Fong/Pittsburgh Post-Gazette; 27R, Courtesy Laura Schumm; 28, © tbkmedia.de/Alamy; 29, © Dave King/Dorling Kindersley/Getty Images; 31L, © Utekhina Anna/Shutterstock; 31R, © Khorkova Olda/Shutterstock; 32, © Darren A. Hubley/Shutterstock.

Publisher: Kenn Goin
Editorial Director: Adam Siegel
Creative Director: Spencer Brinker
Photo Researcher: Jennifer Bright
Design: Dawn Beard Creative

Library of Congress Cataloging-in-Publication Data

Lunis, Natalie.
  Dachshund : the hot dogger / by Natalie Lunis.
    p. cm. — (Little dogs rock!)
  Includes bibliographical references and index.
  ISBN-13: 978-1-59716-744-4 (library binding)
  ISBN-10: 1-59716-744-4 (library binding)
  1. Dachshunds—Juvenile literature. I. Title.

  SF429.D25L59 2009
  636.753'8—dc22
                    2008030829

For more information, write to Bearport Publishing Company, Inc., 101 Fifth Avenue, Suite 6R, New York, New York 10003. Printed in the United States of America.

10 9 8 7 6 5 4 3 2 1

Contents

Ready to Race

On July 14, 2007, a crowd filled the stands of a large racecourse in Los Alamitos, California. More than 12,000 adults and children had gathered to watch the event that was about to begin.

Normally, a group of 1,000-pound (454-kg) racehorses with long, powerful legs would be lined up at the starting gate. Tonight, however, a different kind of animal was getting ready to run.

These **competitors** weighed under 35 pounds (16 kg) and had short legs, sausage-shaped bodies, and a loud bark. They were little dogs called dachshunds (DAHKS-*hunts*)—and they were about to begin a race called the Wiener Nationals.

▼ **Dachshunds racing at the Wiener Nationals**

Fans cheer for their favorite dachshunds.

The Wiener Nationals have been held since 1996 and have become the biggest dachshund race of the year. Smaller dachshund races take place in cities such as Phoenix, Arizona; Kansas City, Kansas; and Cleveland, Ohio.

A Run for Fun

In spite of all the excitement, dachshund races like the Wiener Nationals are not serious sporting events. Instead, they are held for two main purposes. One is to raise money for nearby animal shelters. The other is to give dachshunds and their owners a chance to have fun together.

▲ **Owners stand behind the finish line holding toys and treats to try to get the dachshunds to run in the right direction.**

In 2007, sales of tickets, caps, and T-shirts at the Wiener Nationals raised $20,000 for the Seal Beach Animal Care Center in Southern California.

Often, several of the four-legged athletes don't even finish the race. Some stay back to play with their **rivals**. Others wander off to the **sidelines** to say hello to their fans.

A few dogs, however, always manage to run straight to the finish line. In the Wiener Nationals, the first one across wins a trophy—and the title of the "Fastest Wiener in the West."

▼ The winner of the 2007 Wiener Nationals was Sally. She finished the 150-foot (45.7-m) race in just over seven seconds.

The "Badger Dog"

Today, dachshunds run for fun in races like the Wiener Nationals. In the past, however, they ran while doing serious work. These little dogs chased and cornered badgers.

▲ A badger is a furry mammal that belongs to the weasel family.

The name *dachshund* means "badger dog." In German, *dachs* means "badger," and *hund* means "dog."

In fact, the dachshund got its start as a **breed** during the 1500s in Germany because of badgers. Hunters needed dogs that could follow these weasel-like animals into their underground **burrows**. So they raised small dogs with short legs and long bodies for this job. In the early 1600s, the dogs came to be known as dachshunds.

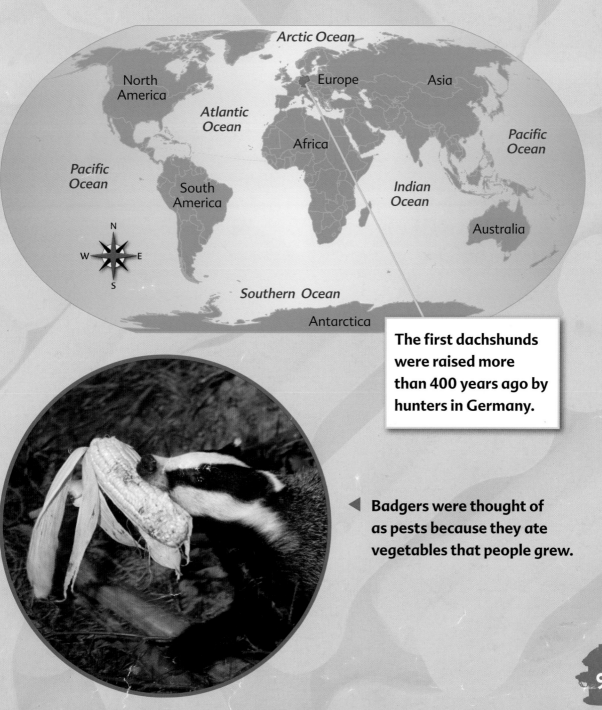

The first dachshunds were raised more than 400 years ago by hunters in Germany.

◀ Badgers were thought of as pests because they ate vegetables that people grew.

Brave, Bold, and Loyal

Hunting badgers was dangerous work for a dachshund. Badgers have sharp, strong claws for digging. When a dachshund trapped one of these animals in its burrow, the badger would try to use them to defend itself. A dachshund had to be brave and **bold** to survive.

No matter how small a dachshund was, it had to be even tougher than its enemy, the badger.

Dachshunds that worked as hunting dogs also had to be intelligent. When chasing a badger, they often ran ahead of the hunters. So they needed to be able to think for themselves until their owners caught up with them. They had to be loyal and trusting, too, in order to work closely with people.

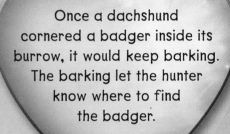

Once a dachshund cornered a badger inside its burrow, it would keep barking. The barking let the hunter know where to find the badger.

Dachshunds are good at digging. ▶
They often had to dig to get into
a badger's burrow.

Different Sizes

People often use nicknames such as "wiener dog," "sausage dog," and "hot dog" for dachshunds because of the shape of their long bodies. All dachshunds are shaped the same way, but they are not all the same size.

Dachshunds come in two different sizes, which are known as standard and miniature. Standard dachshunds weigh between 12 and 32 pounds (5.4 and 14 kg) as adults. Miniatures, which are smaller, weigh 11 pounds (5 kg) or less.

A miniature dachshund (left) and a standard dachshund (right)

People first raised miniature dachshunds in the 1800s in order to help with hunting rabbits. Rabbits are smaller than badgers, and they dig and hide in smaller burrows. So hunters needed smaller-sized dachshunds to catch them.

Different Coats and Colors

Dachshunds don't just come in different sizes. They also come with different kinds of **coats**. There are short-haired dachshunds, long-haired dachshunds, and wire-haired dachshunds.

◀ A short-haired dachshund (also called a smooth-coated dachshund)

A long-haired dachshund ▶

◀ A wire-haired dachshund

At first all dachshunds had short hair. The hunters who raised the dogs noticed a problem, however. Their smooth, short-haired coats did not protect them as they ran through the **shrubs** and bushes that grew in the forest. So the hunters also began to raise dachshunds with long, silky coats and dachshunds with rough, wiry coats. Both of these kinds of coats protected the dogs from getting cut and scratched by **thorns**, sticks, and other sharp objects.

Dachshunds' coats come in many different colors and patterns. Some are solid red, chocolate, or cream. Others are a main color with different-colored patches or stripes.

15

A Pet Fit for a Queen

During the 1800s, hunting was a popular sport for members of **royalty** in many parts of Europe. The dachshund was one of their favorite hunting dogs. One powerful queen, however, helped make the dachshund into a popular pet as well.

Queen Victoria ruled England for more than 60 years, from 1837 to 1901. This photo, taken around 1870, shows her with one of her dachshunds.

In 1840, Queen Victoria of England married a German prince named Albert. Prince Albert brought dachshunds to England with him and gave several of them to the queen as gifts.

Queen Victoria did not use her dachshunds as hunting dogs. Instead, she kept them as pets. Soon many rich people got dachshunds of their own. Eager to be seen keeping up with the latest style, they often walked their trendy pets in the parks of London.

People brought dachshunds to the United States in the 1870s. The dogs quickly became popular pets there, too.

◀ **This monument was put up at Windsor Castle in England. It marks the spot where one of the queen's beloved dachshunds is buried.**

A Top-Ten Pet

The dachshund's liveliness, intelligence, and loyalty made it an outstanding hunting dog. The same qualities also make it an outstanding pet.

Dachshunds love to be with the people who take care of them. They enjoy running and playing outdoors with their owners. Yet they are not happy being left alone outdoors for long periods of time. They'd rather curl up in a cozy spot indoors with their family.

Dachshunds like to be active—but they also like to relax at home.

Since dachshunds are so small, they can make their homes wherever people live. They can keep up with a family living on a farm or on a big ranch. Yet they can also get all the exercise they need exploring a small yard in the suburbs or having fun with other dogs in a city park.

▲ A standard dachshund is easy for most people to tote around town. A miniature is even easier to carry.

Year after year, dachshunds make the top ten list of the most popular dog breeds in the United States.

Dachshund Dos and Don'ts

Dachshunds are lovable pets, but they can present some problems that owners need to watch out for. They can bark nonstop. They can dig lots of holes. They can also run off to chase squirrels and other animals. All these habits work well for hunting dogs but not so well for household pets!

Dachshunds should always be kept on a leash or in a fenced area. Otherwise, they might take off after a squirrel, rabbit, or chipmunk.

Dachshund owners also need to keep a serious **health risk** in mind. Many dachshunds develop back problems. To protect their pets from **injuries**, people need to keep their dachshunds from jumping too high or climbing steep steps.

Dachshunds that are allowed to sit on chairs, sofas, or beds often reach them by using stairs designed for pets. The stairs keep the little dogs from jumping and hurting their backs.

Puppies

When a dachshund puppy is born, it looks very different from an adult. It doesn't have long ears and a long body like its parents. Its **muzzle** is much shorter, too. The puppy begins to look more like an adult after four to six weeks.

A newborn puppy is also different from an adult because it cannot see or hear. Its eyes and ears are closed at first. They open when the puppy is one or two weeks old.

Puppies start to eat solid food at the age of four weeks. Before that, their mother feeds them with milk that she makes in her body.

▲ **A mother dachshund feeding her puppies**

There are usually three to six puppies in a dachshund **litter**. The puppies stay close to their mother until they are about four weeks old. Then, little by little, they start exploring the world. When they are about eight weeks old, they are ready to be **adopted** by a human family.

This dachshund puppy is eight weeks old.

In the Movies

Pet owners aren't the only people who find "wiener dogs" hard to resist. They are popular with moviemakers as well.

Two of the most famous movies that feature dachshunds are *Toy Story* (1995) and *All Dogs Go to Heaven* (1989). In *Toy Story*, the dachshund character is named Slinky. Slinky is a loyal friend to Sheriff Woody—the leader of a group of toys belonging to a little boy named Andy.

Slinky with a toy named Rex in *Toy Story*

The movie character Slinky was based on a real toy called Slinky Dog. The toy was made and sold in the 1950s, 1960s, and early 1970s.

The dachshund in *All Dogs Go to Heaven* is named Itchy Itchiford. Like Slinky, he is a loyal friend to the main character—in this case, a German shepherd named Charlie B. Barkin. Itchy helps save the day when Charlie is captured by his enemy, a pit bull named Carface Carruthers.

▲ **Itchy (left) and Charlie (bottom right) in *All Dogs Go to Heaven***

Wieners on Wheels

For a long time, the dachshund has been known as the hunting dog and family pet with a bold personality. Today, many dachshunds are showing their **independent** and **determined** spirit in a new way. With the help of some special equipment, such as wheelchairs, these dachshunds are overcoming **physical disabilities**.

▲ **This wire-haired dachshund uses a wheelchair cart to help him get around.**

Dachshunds are not the only dogs that use pet wheelchairs. Large dogs such as German shepherds and Dobermans use them, too.

Asher, a short-haired dachshund from Pennsylvania, is one of these spunky **canines**. He was born with a back right leg that was shorter than his left one. Yet that problem hasn't stopped him from getting around. In fact, this wheelchair athlete made headlines in 2007 when he competed in a local "fun run" called the Wiener 100.

Asher didn't win the 100-foot (30-m) race, but he definitely led the way as a crowd favorite. Everyone who watched this hometown hero agreed that he is a real "wiener."

Asher and his owner, ▶
Laura Schumm

Asher was front-page news in Pittsburgh, Pennsylvania, at the time of the race.

Dachshunds at a Glance

Weight:	Standard: 12–32 pounds (5.4–14 kg) Miniature: 11 pounds (5 kg) or less
Height at Shoulder:	Standard: 10–12 inches (25–30 cm) Miniature: 6–8 inches (15–20 cm)
Coat Hair:	Short, wire-haired, or long
Colors:	Some are solid red, chocolate, or cream; others are black, chocolate, or blue (gray) with tan markings on the feet and head and around the tail
Country of Origin:	Germany
Life Span:	12–14 years
Personality:	Brave; feisty; may challenge bigger dogs; likes to hunt; loves to dig and chew; barks a lot

Best in Show

What makes a great dachshund? Every owner knows that his or her dog is special. Judges in dog shows, however, look very carefully at a dachshund's appearance and behavior. Here are some of the things they look for:

ears are near the top of the head and are rounded; they should not be narrow, pointed, or folded

eyes are of a medium size and very dark in color

tail has no kinks or twists

Behavior: should be lively and clever; not shy

neck is long and muscular

back paws are smaller than front paws

Ideal Standard Weight:
16—32 pounds (7—14 kg)

Ideal Miniature Weight:
11 pounds (5 kg) or less

Glossary

adopted (uh-DOPT-id) taken into a family

bold (BOHLD) daring

breed (BREED) a kind of dog

burrows (BUR-ohz) tunnels made by animals to use as homes or hiding places

canines (KAY-nyenz) members of the dog family, including pet dogs, wolves, foxes, and coyotes

coats (KOHTS) the fur on dogs or other animals

competitors (kuhm-PET-i-turz) animals or people taking part in a contest or sporting event

determined (di-TUR-mind) having a strong will to do something

health risk (HELTH RISK) a physical condition that increases the likelihood of an illness or accident

independent (*in*-di-PEN-duhnt) able to do things without needing help from others

injuries (IN-jur-eez) harm

litter (LIT-ur) a group of baby animals, such as puppies or kittens, that are born to the same mother at the same time

muzzle (MUHZ-uhl) the nose, mouth, and jaws of an animal

physical disabilities (FIZ-uh-kuhl *diss*-uh-BILL-uh-teez) conditions that make it hard for a person or animal to do everyday things such as walking, seeing, or hearing

rivals (RYE-vuhlz) animals or people that compete against other animals or people

royalty (ROY-uhl-tee) kings, queens, princes, and princesses

shrubs (SHRUHBS) plants that have many woody stems

sidelines (SIDE-lyenz) the area that is just outside of the place where a sport is played

thorns (THORNZ) sharp points on the branches or stems of some plants

Bibliography

Gordon, Ann. *Dachshund.* 2nd ed. Hoboken, NJ: Howell Book House (2005).

Schwartz, Ingrid. *Dachshund.* Allenhurst, NJ: Kennel Club Books (2004).

Walker, Joan Hustace. *The Everything Dachshund Book: A Complete Guide to Raising, Training, and Caring for Your Dachshund.* Avon, MA: Adams Media (2005).

Read More

Heyman, Anita. *Gretchen: The Bicycle Dog.* New York: Dutton Children's Books (2003).

Quasha, Jennifer. *The Story of the Dachshund.* New York: PowerKids Press (2000).

Stone, Lynn M. *Dachshunds.* Vero Beach, FL: Rourke Publishing (2003).

Wilcox, Charlotte. *The Dachshund.* Mankato, MN: Captsone Press (2001).

Learn More Online

To learn more about dachshunds, visit
www.bearportpublishing.com/LittleDogsRock

Index

About the Author

Natalie Lunis has written many science and nature books for children. She lives in the Hudson River Valley, just north of New York City.